The Practice of the Presence of GOD

BROTHER LAWRENCE

GENERAL PRESS

Published by

GENERAL PRESS

4805/24, Fourth Floor, Krishna House
Ansari Road, Daryaganj, New Delhi - 110002
Ph : 011-23282971, 45795759
E-mail : generalpressindia@gmail.com

www.generalpress.in

First Edition : 2022

ISBN : 9789354993879

Published by Azeem Ahmad Khan for General Press

Contents

Preface

"I believe in the... communion of saints."

Surely if additional proof of its reality were needed, it might be found in the universal oneness of experimental Christianity in all ages and in all lands. The experiences of Thomas á Kempis, of Tauler and of Madame Guyon, of John Woolman and Hester Ann Rogers, how marvellously they agree, and how perfectly they harmonize! And Nicholas Herman, of Lorraine, whose letters and converse are here given, testifies to the same truth! In communion with Rome, a lay brother among the Carmelites, for several years a soldier, in an irreligious age, amid a sceptical people, yet in him the practice of the presence of GOD was as much a reality as the "watch" of the early Friends, and the "holy seed" in him and others was the "stock" (Isa. vi. 13) from which grew the household and evangelistic piety of the eighteenth century, of Epworth and of Moorfields.

"When unadorned, adorned the most" is the line which deters from any interpolations or interpretations other than the few "contents" headings which are given. May the "Christ in you" be the "hope of glory" to all who read.

Conversations

First Conversation

*Conversion and previous employment. * Satisfaction in God's presence. * Faith our duty. * Resignation the fruit of watchfulness.*

The first time I saw Brother Lawrence was upon the 3rd of August, 1666. He told me that GOD had done him a singular favour, in his conversion at the age of eighteen.

That in the winter, seeing a tree stripped of its leaves, and considering that within a little time, the leaves would be renewed, and after that the flowers and fruit appear, he received a high view of the Providence and Power of GOD, which has never since been effaced from his soul. That this view had perfectly set him loose from the world, and kindled in him such a love for GOD, that he could not tell whether it had increased in above forty years that he had lived since.

That he had been footman to M. Fieubert, the treasurer, and that he was a great awkward fellow who broke everything.

That he had desired to be received into a monastery, thinking that he would there be made to smart for his awkwardness and the faults he should commit, and so he should sacrifice to GOD his life, with its pleasures: but that GOD had disappointed him, he having met with nothing but satisfaction in that state.

That we should establish ourselves in a sense of GOD's Presence, by continually conversing with Him. That it was a shameful thing to quit His conversation, to think of trifles and fooleries.

That we should feed and nourish our souls with high notions of GOD; which would yield us great joy in being devoted to Him.

That we ought to quicken, i.e., to enliven, our faith. That it was lamentable we had so little; and that instead of taking faith for the rule of their conduct, men amused themselves with trivial devotions, which changed daily. That the way of Faith was the spirit of the Church, and that it was sufficient to bring us to a high degree of perfection.

That we ought to give ourselves up to GOD, with regard both to things temporal and spiritual, and seek our satisfaction only in the fulfilling of His will, whether He lead us by suffering or by consolation, for all would be equal to a soul truly resigned. That there needed fidelity in those drynesses, or insensibilities and irksomenesses in prayer, by which GOD tries our love to Him; that then was the time for us to make good and effectual acts of resignation, whereof one alone would oftentimes very much promote our spiritual advancement.

That as for the miseries and sins he heard of daily in the world, he was so far from wondering at them, that, on the contrary, he was surprised there were not more, considering the malice sinners were capable of: that for his part, he prayed for them; but knowing that GOD could remedy the mischief's they did, when He pleased, he gave himself no further trouble.

That to arrive at such resignation as GOD requires, we should watch attentively over all the passions which mingle as well in spiritual things as those of a grosser nature: that GOD would give light concerning those passions to those who truly desire to serve Him. That if this was my design, viz., sincerely to serve GOD, I might come to him (Bro. Lawrence) as often as I pleased, without any fear of being troublesome; but if not, that I ought no more to visit him.

Second Conversation

*Love the motive of all. * Once in fear, now in joy. * Diligence and love. Simplicity the key to Divine assistance. * Business abroad as at home. * Times of prayer and self-mortification not essential for the practice. * All scruples brought to God.*

That he had always been governed by love, without selfish views; and that having resolved to make the love of GOD the end of all his actions, he had found reasons to be well satisfied with his method. That he was pleased when he could take up a straw from the ground for the love of GOD, seeking Him only, and nothing else, not even His gifts.

That he had been long troubled in mind from a certain belief that he should be damned; that all the men in the world could not have persuaded him to the contrary; but that he had thus reasoned with himself about it: I did not engage in a religious life but for the love of GOD, and I have endeavoured to act only for Him; whatever becomes of me, whether I be lost or saved, I will always continue to act purely for the love of GOD. I shall have this good at least, that till death I shall have done all that is in me to love Him. That this trouble of mind had lasted four years; during which time he had suffered much.

That since that time he had passed his life in perfect liberty and continual joy. That he placed his sins betwixt him and GOD, as it were, to tell Him that he did not deserve His favours, but that GOD still continued to bestow them in abundance.

That in order to form a habit of conversing with GOD continually, and referring all we do to Him; we must at first apply to Him with some diligence: but that after a little care we should find His love inwardly excite us to it without any difficulty.

That he expected after the pleasant days GOD had given him, he should have his turn of pain and suffering; but that he was not uneasy about it, knowing very well, that as he could do nothing of himself, GOD would not fail to give him the strength to bear them.

That when an occasion of practising some virtue offered, he addressed himself to GOD, saying, LORD, I cannot do this unless Thou enablest me; and that then he received strength more than sufficient.

That when he had failed in his duty, he only confessed his fault, saying to GOD, I shall never do otherwise, if You leave me to myself; 'tis You must hinder my falling, and mend what is amiss. That after this, he gave himself no further uneasiness about it.

That we ought to act with GOD in the greatest simplicity, speaking to Him frankly and plainly, and imploring His assistance in our affairs, just as they happen. That GOD never failed to grant it, as he had often experienced.

That he had been lately sent into Burgundy, to buy the provision of wine for the society, which was a very unwelcome task for him, because he had no turn for business and because he was lame, and could not go about the boat but by rolling himself over the casks. That however he gave himself no uneasiness about it, nor about the purchase of the wine. That he said to GOD, It was His business he was about, and that he afterwards found it very well performed. That he had been sent into Auvergne the year before upon the same account; that he could not tell how the matter passed, but that it proved very well.

So, likewise, in his business in the kitchen (to which he had naturally a great aversion), having accustomed himself to do everything there for the love of GOD, and with prayer, upon all occasions, for His grace to do his work well, he had found everything easy, during the fifteen years that he had been employed there.

That he was very well pleased with the post he was now in; but that he was as ready to quit that as the former, since he was always pleasing himself in every condition, by doing little things for the love of GOD.

That with him the set times of prayer were not different from other times: that he retired to pray, according to the directions of his Superior, but that he did not want such retirement. nor ask for it, because his greatest business did not divert him from GOD.

That as he knew his obligation to love GOD in all things, and as he endeavoured so to do, he had no need of a director to advise him, but that he needed much a confessor to absolve him. That he was very sensible of his faults, but not discouraged by them; that he confessed them to GOD, and did not plead against Him to excuse them. When he had so done, he peaceably resumed his usual practice of love and adoration.

That in his trouble of mind, he had consulted nobody, but knowing only by the light of faith that GOD was present, he contented himself with directing all his actions to Him, i.e., doing them with a desire to please Him, let what would come of it.

That useless thoughts spoil all: that the mischief began there; but that we ought to reject them, as soon as we perceived their impertinence to the matter in hand, or our salvation; and return to our communion with GOD.

That at the beginning he had often passed his time appointed for prayer, in rejecting wandering thoughts, and falling back into them. That he could never regulate his devotion by certain methods as some do. That nevertheless, at first he had meditated for some time, but afterwards that went off, in a manner that he could give no account of.

That all bodily mortifications and other exercises are useless, but as they serve to arrive at the union with GOD by love; that he had well considered this, and found it the shortest way to go straight to Him by a continual exercise of love, and doing all things for His sake.

That we ought to make a great difference between the acts of the understanding and those of the will; that the first were comparatively of little value, and the others all.

That our only business was to love and delight ourselves in GOD.

That all possible kinds of mortification, if they were void of the love of GOD, could not efface a single sin. That we ought, without anxiety, to expect the pardon of our sins from the Blood of JESUS CHRIST, only endeavouring to love Him with all our hearts. That GOD seemed to have granted the greatest favours to the greatest sinners, as more signal monuments of His mercy.

That the greatest pains or pleasures, of this world, were not to be compared with what he had experienced of both kinds in a spiritual state: so that he was careful for nothing and feared nothing, desiring but one only thing of GOD, viz., that he might not offend Him.

That he had no scruples; for, said he, when I fail in my duty, I readily acknowledge it, saying, I am used to do so: I shall never do otherwise, if I am left to myself. If I fail not, then I give GOD thanks, acknowledging that it comes from Him.

Third Conversation

*Faith working by love. * Outward business no detriment. * Perfect resignation the sure way.*

He told me, that the foundation of the spiritual life in him had been a high notion and esteem of GOD in faith; which when he had once well conceived, he had no other care at first, but faithfully to reject every other thought, that he might perform all his actions for the love of GOD. That when sometimes he had not thought of GOD for a good while, he did not disquiet himself for it; but after having acknowledged his wretchedness to GOD, he returned to Him with so much the greater trust in Him, by how much he found himself more wretched to have forgot Him.

That the trust we put in GOD honours Him much, and draws down great graces.

That it was impossible, not only that GOD should deceive, but also that He should long let a soul suffer which is perfectly resigned to Him, and resolved to endure everything for His sake.

That he had so often experienced the ready succours of Divine Grace upon all occasions, that from the same experience, when he had business to do, he did not think of it beforehand; but when it was time to do it, he found in GOD, as in a clear mirror, all that was fit for him to do. That of late he had acted thus, without anticipating care; but before the experience above mentioned, he had used it in his affairs.

When outward business diverted him a little from the thought of GOD, a fresh remembrance coming from GOD invested his soul, and so inflamed and transported him that it was difficult for him to contain himself.

That he was more united to GOD in his outward employments, than when he left them for devotion in retirement.

That he expected hereafter some great pain of body or mind; that the worst that could happen to him was, to lose that sense of GOD, which he had enjoyed so long; but that the goodness of GOD assured him He would not forsake him utterly, and that He would give him strength to bear whatever evil He permitted to happen to him; and therefore that he feared nothing, and had no occasion to consult with anybody about his state. That when he had attempted to do it, he had always come away more perplexed; and that as he was conscious of his readiness to lay down his life for the love of GOD, he had no apprehension of danger. That perfect resignation to GOD was a sure way to heaven, a way in which we had always sufficient light for our conduct.

That in the beginning of the spiritual life, we ought to be faithful in doing our duty and denying ourselves; but after that unspeakable pleasures followed: that in difficulties we need only have recourse to JESUS CHRIST, and beg His grace, with which everything became easy.

That many do not advance in the Christian progress, because they stick in penances, and particular exercises, while they neglect the love of GOD, which is the end. That this appeared plainly by their works, and was the reason why we see so little solid virtue.

That there needed neither art nor science for going to GOD, but only a heart resolutely determined to apply itself to nothing but Him, or for His sake, and to love Him only.

Fourth Conversation

*The manner of going to God. * Hearty renunciation. * Prayer and praise prevent discouragement. * Sanctification in common business. * Prayer and the presence of God. * The whole substance of religion. * Self-estimation * Further personal experience.*

He discoursed with me very frequently, and with great openness of heart, concerning his manner of going to GOD, whereof some part is related already.

He told me, that all consists in one hearty renunciation of everything which we are sensible does not lead to GOD; that we might accustom ourselves to a continual conversation with Him, with freedom and in simplicity. That we need only to recognize GOD intimately present with us, to address ourselves to Him every moment, that we may be His assistance for knowing His will in things doubtful, and for rightly performing those which we plainly see He requires of us, offering them to Him before we do them, and giving Him thanks when we have done.

That in this conversation with GOD, we are also employed in praising, adoring, and loving him incessantly, for His infinite goodness and perfection.

That, without being discouraged on account of our sins, we should pray for His grace with a perfect confidence, as relying upon the infinite merits of our LORD. That GOD never failed offering us His grace at each action; that he distinctly perceived it, and never failed of it, unless when his thoughts had wandered from a sense of GOD's Presence, or he had forgot to ask His assistance.

That GOD always gave us light in our doubts, when we had no other design but to please Him.

That our sanctification did not depend upon changing our works, but in doing that for GOD's sake, which we commonly do for our own. That it was lamentable to see how many people mistook the means for the end, addicting themselves to certain works, which they performed very imperfectly, by reason of their human or selfish regards.

That the most excellent method he had found of going to GOD, was that of doing our common business without any view of pleasing men, [Gal. I. 10; Eph. vi. 5, 6.] and (as far as we are capable) purely for the love of GOD.

That it was a great delusion to think that the times of prayer ought to differ from other times. That we are as strictly obliged to adhere to GOD by action in the time of action, as by prayer in its season.

That his prayer was nothing else but a sense of the presence of GOD, his soul being at that time insensible to everything but Divine love: and that when the appointed times of prayer were past, he found no difference, because he still continued with GOD, praising and blessing Him with all his might, so that he passed his life in continual joy; yet hoped that GOD would give him somewhat to suffer, when he should grow stronger.

That we ought, once for all, heartily to put our whole trust in GOD, and make a total surrender of ourselves to Him, secure that He would not deceive us.

That we ought not to be weary of doing little things for the love of GOD, who regards not the greatness of the work, but the love with which it is performed. That we should not wonder if, in the beginning, we often failed in our endeavours, but that at last we should gain a habit, which will naturally produce its acts in us, without our care, and to our exceeding great delight.

That the whole substance of religion was faith, hope, and charity; by the practice of which we become united to the will of GOD: that all beside is indifferent and to be used as a means, that we may arrive at our end, and be swallowed up therein, by faith and charity.

That all things are possible to him who believes, that they are less difficult to him who hopes, they are more easy to him who loves, and still more easy to him who perseveres in the practice of these three virtues.

That the end we ought to propose to ourselves is to become, in this life, the most perfect worshippers of GOD we can possibly be, as we hope to be through all eternity.

That when we enter upon the spiritual we should consider, and examine to the bottom, what we are. And then we should find ourselves worthy of all contempt, and such as do not deserve the name of Christians, subject to all kinds of misery, and numberless accidents, which trouble us, and cause perpetual vicissitudes in our health, in our humours, in our internal and external dispositions: in fine, persons whom GOD would humble by many pains and labours, as well within as without. After this, we should not wonder that troubles, temptations, oppositions and contradictions, happen to us from men. We ought, on the contrary, to submit ourselves to them, and bear them as long as GOD pleases, as things highly advantageous to us.

That the greater perfection a soul aspires after, the more dependent it is upon Divine grace.

Being questioned by one of his own society (to whom he was obliged to open himself) by what means he had attained such an habitual sense of GOD? he told him that, since his first coming to the monastery, he had considered GOD as the end of all his thoughts and desires, as the mark to which they should tend, and in which they should terminate.

That in the beginning of his novitiate he spent the hours appointed for private prayer in thinking of GOD, so as to convince his mind of, and to impress deeply upon his heart, the Divine existence, rather by devout sentiments, and submission to the lights of faith, than by studied reasoning's and elaborate meditations. That by this short and sure method, he exercised himself in the knowledge and love of GOD, resolving to use his utmost endeavour to live in a continual sense of His Presence, and, if possible, never to forget Him more.

That when he had thus in prayer filled his mind with great sentiments of that infinite Being, he went to his work appointed in the kitchen (for he was cook to the society); there having first considered severally the things his office required, and when and how each thing was to be done, he spent all the intervals of his time, as well before as after his work, in prayer.

That, when he began his business, he said to GOD, with a filial trust in Him, "O my GOD, since Thou art with me, and I must now, in obedience to Thy commands, apply my mind to these outward things, I beseech Thee to grant me the grace to continue in Thy Presence; and to this end do Thou prosper me with Thy assistance, receive all my works, and possess all my affections."

As he proceeded in his work, he continued his familiar conversation with his Maker, imploring His grace, and offering to Him all his actions.

When he had finished, he examined himself how he had discharged his duty; if he found well, he returned thanks to GOD; if otherwise, he asked pardon; and without being discouraged, he set his mind right again, and continued his exercise of the presence of GOD, as if he had never deviated from it. "Thus," said he, "by rising after my falls, and by frequently renewed acts of faith and love, I am come to a state, wherein it would be as difficult for me not to think of GOD, as it was at first to accustom myself to it."

As Bro. Lawrence had found such an advantage in walking in the presence of GOD, it was natural for him to recommend it earnestly to others; but his example was a stronger inducement than any arguments he could propose. His very countenance was edifying; such a sweet and calm devotion appearing in it, as could not but affect the beholders. And it was observed, that in the greatest hurry of business in the kitchen, he still preserved his recollection and heavenly-mindedness. He was never hasty nor loitering, but did each thing in its season, with an even uninterrupted composure and tranquillity of spirit. "The time of business," said he, "does not with me differ from the time of prayer; and in the noise and clutter of my kitchen, while several persons are at the same time calling for different things, I possess GOD in as great tranquillity as if I were upon my knees at the Blessed Sacrament."

Letters

First Letter

How the habitual sense of God's Presence was found.

Since you desire so earnestly that I should communicate to you the method by which I arrived at that habitual sense of GOD's Presence, which our LORD, of His mercy, has been pleased to vouchsafe to me; I must tell you, that it is with great difficulty that I am prevailed on by your importunities; and now I do it only upon the terms, that you show my letter to nobody. If I knew that you would let it be seen, all the desire that I have for your advancement would not be able to determine me to it. The account I can give you is:

Having found in many books different methods of going to GOD, and divers practices of the spiritual life, I thought this would serve rather to puzzle me, than facilitate what

I sought after, which was nothing but how to become wholly GOD's.

This made me resolve to give the all for the All: so after having given myself wholly to GOD, to make all the satisfaction I could for my sins, I renounced, for the love of Him, everything that was not He; and I began to live as if there was none but He and I in the world. Sometimes I considered myself before Him as a poor criminal at the feet of his judge; at other times I beheld Him in my heart as my FATHER, as my GOD: I worshipped Him the oftenest that I could, keeping my mind in His holy Presence, and recalling it as often as I found it wandered from Him. I found no small pain in this exercise, and yet I continued it, notwithstanding all the difficulties that occurred, without troubling or disquieting myself when my mind had wandered involuntarily. I made this my business, as much all the day long as at the appointed times of prayer; for at all times, every hour, every minute, even in the height of my business, I drove away from my mind everything that was capable of interrupting my thought of GOD.

Such has been my common practice ever since I entered into religion; and though I have done it very imperfectly, yet I have found great advantages by it. These, I well know, are to be imputed to the mere mercy and goodness of GOD, because we can do nothing without Him; and I still less than any. But when we are faithful to keep ourselves in His holy Presence, and set Him always before us, this not only hinders our offending Him, and doing anything that may displease Him, at least wilfully, but it also begets in us a holy freedom, and if I may so speak, a familiarity with GOD, wherewith we ask, and that successfully, the graces we stand in need of. In fine, by often repeating these acts, they become habitual, and the presence of GOD is rendered as it were natural to us. Give Him thanks, if you please, with me, for His great goodness towards me, which I can never sufficiently admire, for the many favours He has done to so miserable a sinner as I am. May all things praise Him. Amen.

Second Letter

*Difference between himself and others. * Faith alone consistently and persistently. * Deprecates this state being considered a delusion.*

Not finding my manner of life in books, although I have no difficulty about it, yet, for greater security, I shall be glad to know your thoughts concerning it.

In a conversation some days since with a person of piety, he told me the spiritual life was a life of grace, which begins with servile fear, which is increased by hope of eternal life, and which is consummated by pure love; that each of these states had its different stages, by which one arrives at last at that blessed consummation.

I have not followed all these methods. On the contrary, from I know not what instincts, I found they discouraged me. This was the reason why, at my entrance into religion, I took a resolution to give myself up to GOD, as the best satisfaction I could make for my sins; and, for the love of Him, to renounce all besides.

For the first years, I commonly employed myself during the time set apart for devotion, with the thoughts of death, judgement, hell, heaven, and my sins. Thus I continued some years applying my mind carefully the rest of the day, and even in the midst of my business, to the presence of GOD, whom I considered always as with me, often as in me.

At length I came insensibly to do the same thing during my set time of prayer, which caused in me great delight and consolation. This practice produced in me so high an esteem for GOD, that faith alone was capable to satisfy me in that point. [I suppose he means that all distinct notions he could form of GOD were unsatisfactory, because he perceived them to be unworthy of GOD, and therefore his mind was not to be satisfied but by the views of faith, which apprehends GOD as infinite and incomprehensible, as He is in Himself, and not as He can be conceived by human ideas.]

Such was my beginning; and yet I must tell you, that for the first ten years I suffered much: the apprehension that I was not devoted to GOD, as I wished to be, my past sins always present to my mind, and the great unmerited favours which GOD did me, were the matter and source of my sufferings. During this time I fell often, and rose again presently. It seemed to me that the creatures, reason, and GOD Himself were against me; And faith alone for me. I was troubled sometimes with thoughts, that to believe I had received such favours was an effect of my presumption, which pretended to be at once where others arrive with difficulty; at other times that it was a wilful delusion, and that there was no salvation for me.

When I thought of nothing but to end my days in these troubles (which did not at all diminish the trust I had in GOD, and which served only to increase my faith), I found myself changed all at once; and my soul, which till that time was in trouble, felt a profound inward peace, as if she were in her centre and place of rest.

Ever since that time I walk before GOD simply, in faith, with humility and with love; and I apply myself diligently to do nothing and think nothing which may displease Him. I hope that when I have done what I can, He will do with me what He pleases.

As for what passes in me at present, I cannot express it. I have no pain or difficulty about my state, because I have no will but that of GOD, which I endeavour to accomplish in all things, and to which I am so resigned, that I would not take up a straw from the ground against His order, or from any other motive but purely that of love to Him.

I have quitted all forms of devotion and set prayers but those to which my state obliges me. And I make it my business only to persevere in His holy presence, wherein I keep myself by a simple attention, and a general fond regard to GOD, which I may call an actual presence of GOD; or, to speak better, an habitual, silent, and secret conversation of the soul with GOD, which often causes in me joys and raptures inwardly, and sometimes also outwardly, so great that I am forced to use means to moderate them, and prevent their appearance to others.

In short, I am assured beyond all doubt, that my soul has been with GOD above these thirty years. I pass over many things, that I may not be tedious to you, yet I think it proper to inform you after what manner I consider myself before GOD, whom I behold as my King.

I consider myself as the most wretched of men, full of sores and corruption, and who has committed all sorts of crimes against his King; touched with a sensible regret I confess to Him all my wickedness, I ask His forgiveness, I abandon myself in His hands, that He may do what He pleases with me. This King, full of mercy and goodness, very far from chastising me, embraces me with love, makes me eat at His table, serves me with His own hands, gives me the key of His treasures; He converses and delights Himself with me incessantly, in a thousand and a thousand ways, and treats me in all respects as His favourite. It is thus I consider myself from time to time in His holy presence.

My most usual method is this simple attention, and such a general passionate regard to GOD; to whom I find myself often attached with greater sweetness and delight than that of an infant at the mother's breast: so that if I dare use the expression, I should choose to call this state the bosom of GOD, for the inexpressible sweetness which I taste and experience there. If sometimes my thoughts wander from it by necessity or infirmity, I am presently recalled by inward motions, so charming and delicious that I am ashamed to mention them.

I desire your reverence to reflect rather upon my great wretchedness, of which you are fully informed, than upon the great favours which GOD does me, all unworthy and ungrateful as I am.

As for my set hours of prayer, they are only a continuation of the same exercise. Sometimes I consider myself there, as a stone before a carver, whereof he is to make a statue: presenting myself thus before GOD, I desire Him to make His perfect image in my soul, and render me entirely like Himself.

At other times, when I apply myself to prayer, I feel all my spirit and all my soul lift itself up without any care or effort of mine; and it continues as it were suspended and firmly fixed in GOD, as in its centre and place of rest.

I know that some charge this state with inactivity, delusion, and self-love: I confess that it is a holy inactivity, and would be a happy self-love, if the soul in that state were capable of it; because in effect, while she is in this repose, she cannot be disturbed by such acts as she was formerly accustomed to, and which were then her support, but would now rather hinder than assist her.

Yet I cannot bear that this should be called delusion; because the soul which thus enjoys GOD desires herein nothing but Him. If this be delusion in me, it belongs to GOD to remedy it. Let Him do what He pleases with me: I desire only Him, and to be wholly devoted to Him.

You will, however, oblige me in sending me your opinion, to which I always pay a great deference, for I have a singular esteem for your reverence, and am yours in our Lord.

Third Letter

For a soldier friend whom he encourages to trust in God.

We have a GOD who is infinitely gracious, and knows all our wants. I always thought that He would reduce you to extremity. He will come in His own time, and when you least expect it. Hope in Him more than ever: thank Him with me for the favours He does you, particularly for the fortitude and patience which He gives you in your afflictions: it is a plain mark of the care He takes of you; comfort yourself then with Him, and give thanks for all.

I admire also the fortitude and bravery of M. GOD has given him a good disposition, and a good will; but there is in him still a little of the world, and a great deal of youth. I hope the affliction which GOD has sent him will prove a wholesome remedy to him, and make him enter into himself; it is an accident very proper to engage him to put all his trust in Him, who accompanies him everywhere: let him think of Him the oftenest he can, especially in the greatest dangers. A little lifting up the heart suffices; a little remembrance of GOD, one act of inward worship, though upon a march, and sword in hand, are prayers which, however short, are nevertheless very acceptable to GOD; and far from lessening a soldier's courage in occasions of danger, they best serve to fortify it.

Let him then think of GOD the most he can; let him accustom himself, by degrees, to this small but holy exercise; nobody perceives it, and nothing is easier than to repeat often in the day these little internal adorations. Recommend to him, if you please, that he think of GOD the most he can, in the manner here directed; it is very fit and most necessary for a soldier, who is daily exposed to dangers of life, and often of his salvation. I hope that GOD will assist him and all the family, to whom I present my service, being theirs and yours.

Fourth Letter

Writes of himself as of a third person, and encourages his correspondent to press on to fuller practising of the Presence of God.

I have taken this opportunity to communicate to you the sentiments of one of our society concerning the admirable effects and continual assistances which he receives from the presence of GOD. Let you and me both profit by them.

You must know, his continual care has been, for above forty years past that he has spent in religion, to be always with GOD; and to do nothing, say nothing, and think nothing which may displease Him; and this without any other view than purely for the love of Him, and because He deserves infinitely more.

He is now so accustomed to that Divine presence, that he receives from it continual succours upon all occasions. For about thirty years, his soul has been filled with joys so continual, and sometimes so great, that he is forced to use means to moderate them, and to hinder their appearing outwardly.

If sometimes he is a little too much absent from that Divine presence, GOD presently makes Himself to be felt in his soul to recall him; which often happens when he is most engaged in his outward business: he answers with exact fidelity to these inward drawings, either by an elevation of his heart towards GOD, or by a meek and fond regard to Him, or by such words as love forms upon these occasions; as for instance, My GOD, here I am all devoted to Thee: LORD, make me according to Thy heart. And then it seems to him (as in effect he feels it) that this GOD of love, satisfied with such few words, reposes again, and rests in the depth and centre of his soul. The experience of these things gives him such an assurance that GOD is always in the depth or bottom of his soul, and renders him incapable of doubting it, upon any account whatever.

Judge by this what content and satisfaction he enjoys, while he continually finds in himself so great a treasure: he is no longer in an anxious search after it, but has it open before him, and may take what he pleases of it.

He complains much of our blindness; and cries often that we are to be pitied who content ourselves with so little. GOD, saith he, has infinite treasure to bestow, and we take up with a little sensible devotion which passes in a moment. Blind as we are, we hinder GOD, and stop the current of His graces. But when He finds a soul penetrated with a lively faith, He pours into it His graces and favours plentifully; there they flow like a torrent, which, after being forcibly stopped against its ordinary course, when it has found a passage, spreads itself with impetuosity and abundance.

Yes, we often stop this torrent, by the little value we set upon it. But let us stop it no more: let us enter into ourselves and break down the bank which hinders it. Let us make way for grace; let us redeem the lost time, for perhaps we have but little left; death follows us close, let us be well prepared for it; for we die but once, and a miscarriage there is irretrievable.

I say again, let us enter into ourselves. The time presses: there is no room for delay; our souls are at stake. I believe you have taken such effectual measures, that you will not be surprised. I commend you for it, it is the one thing necessary: we must, nevertheless, always work at it, because not to advance, in the spiritual life, is to go back. But those who have the gale of the HOLY SPIRIT go forward even in sleep. If the vessel of our soul is still tossed with winds and storms, let us awake the LORD, who reposes in it, and He will quickly calm the sea.

I have taken the liberty to impart to you these good sentiments, that you may compare them with your own: they will serve again to kindle and inflame them, if by misfortune (which GOD forbid, for it would be indeed a great misfortune) they should be, though never so little, cooled. Let us then both recall our first fervours. Let us profit by the example and the sentiments of this brother, who is little known of the world, but known of GOD, and extremely caressed by Him. I will pray for you; do you pray instantly for me, who am yours in our LORD.

Fifth Letter

*Prayer for a sister who is about to make a vow and profession. * A fresh insisting upon the necessity and virtue of practising the Presence of God.*

I received this day two books and a letter from Sister, who is preparing to make her profession, and upon that account desires the prayers of your holy society, and yours in particular. I perceive that she reckons much upon them; pray do not disappoint her. Beg of GOD that she may make her sacrifice in the view of His love alone, and with a firm resolution to be wholly devoted to Him.

I will send you one of those books which treat of the presence of GOD; a subject which, in my opinion, contains the whole spiritual life; and it seems to me that whoever duly practises it will soon become spiritual.

I know that for the right practice of it, the heart must be empty of all other things; because GOD will possess the heart alone; and as He cannot possess it alone, without emptying it of all besides, so neither can He act there, and do in it what He pleases, unless it be left vacant to Him.

There is not in the world a kind of life more sweet and delightful, than that of a continual conversation with GOD: those only can comprehend it who practise and experience it; yet I do not advise you to do it from that motive; it is not pleasure which we ought to seek in this exercise; but let us do it from a principle of love, and because GOD would have us.

Were I a preacher, I should above all other things preach the practice of the presence of GOD; and were I a director, I should advise all the world to do it: so necessary do I think it, and so easy too.

Ah! knew we but they want we have of the grace and assistance of GOD, we should never lose sight of Him, no, not for a moment. Believe me; make immediately a holy and firm resolution never more wilfully to forget Him, and to spend the rest of your days in His sacred presence, deprived for the love of Him, if He thinks fit, of all consolations.

Set heartily about this work, and if you do it as you ought, be assured that you will soon find the effects of it. I will assist you with my prayers, poor as they are: I recommend myself earnestly to yours, and those of your holy society.

Sixth Letter

*To a member of the order who had received from him a book, and to whom he again enlarges on his favourite topic. * Encouragement to persevere.*

I have received from Mrs. – the things which you gave her for me. I wonder that you have not given me your thoughts of the little book I sent to you, and which you must have received. Pray set heartily about the practice of it in your old age; it is better late than never.

I cannot imagine how religious persons can live satisfied without the practice of the presence of GOD. For my part I keep myself retired with Him in the depth of centre of my soul as much as I can; and while I am so with Him I fear nothing; but the least turning from Him is insupportable.

This exercise does not much fatigue the body: it is, however, proper to deprive it sometimes, nay often, of many little pleasures which are innocent and lawful: for GOD will not permit that a soul which desires to be devoted entirely to Him should take other pleasures than with Him; that is more than reasonable.

I do not say that therefore we must put any violent constraint upon ourselves. No, we must serve GOD in a holy freedom, we must do our business faithfully, without trouble or disquiet; recalling our mind to GOD mildly and with tranquillity, as often as we find it wandering from Him.

It is, however, necessary to put our whole trust in GOD, laying aside all other cares, and even some particular forms of devotion, though very good in themselves, yet such as one often engages in unreasonably: because those devotions are only means to attain to the end; so when by this exercise of the presence of GOD we are with Him who is our end, it is then useless to return to the means; but we may continue with Him our commerce of love, persevering in His holy presence: one while by an act of praise, of adoration, or of desire; one while by an act of resignation, or thanksgiving; and in all the manner which our spirit can invent.

Be not discouraged by the repugnance which you may find in it from nature; you must do yourself violence. At the first, one often thinks it lost time; but you must go on, and resolve to persevere in it to death, notwithstanding all the difficulties that may occur. I recommend myself to the prayers of your holy society, and yours in particular. I am yours in our LORD.

Seventh Letter

At the age of nearly fourscore exhorts his correspondent, who is sixty-four, to live and die with God and promises and asks for prayer.

I pity you much. It will be of great importance if you can leave the care of your affairs to, and spend the remainder of your life only in worshiping GOD. He requires no great matters of us; a little remembrance of Him from time to time, a little adoration: sometimes to pray for His grace, sometimes to offer Him your sufferings, and sometimes to return Him thanks for the favours He has given you, and still gives you, in the midst of your troubles, and to console yourself with Him the oftenest you can. Lift up your heart to Him, sometimes even at your meals, and when you are in company: the least little remembrance will always be acceptable to Him. You need not cry very loud; He is nearer to us than we are aware of.

It is not necessary for being with GOD to be always at church; we may make an oratory of our heart, wherein to retire from time to time, to converse with Him in meekness, humility, and love. Everyone is capable of such familiar conversation with GOD, some more, some less: He knows what we can do. Let us begin then; perhaps He expects but one generous resolution on our part. Have courage. We have but little time to live; you are near sixty-four, and I am almost eighty. Let us live and die with GOD: sufferings will be sweet and pleasant to us, while we are with Him: and the greatest pleasures will be, without Him, a cruel punishment to us. May He be blessed for all. Amen.

Use yourself then by degrees thus to worship Him, to beg His grace, to offer Him your heart from time to time, in the midst of your business, even every moment if you can. Do not always scrupulously confine yourself to certain rules, or particular forms of devotion; but act with a general confidence in GOD, with love and humility. You may assure – of my poor prayers, and that I am their servant, and yours particularly.

Eighth Letter

Concerning wandering thoughts in prayer.

You tell me nothing new: you are not the only one that is troubled with wandering thoughts. Our mind is extremely roving; but as the will is mistress of all our faculties, she must recall them, and carry them to GOD, as their last end.

When the mind, for want of being sufficiently reduced by recollection, at our first engaging in devotion, has contracted certain bad habits of wandering and dissipation, they are difficult to overcome, and commonly draw us, even against our wills, to the things of the earth.

I believe one remedy for this is, to confess our faults, and to humble ourselves before GOD. I do not advise you to use multiplicity of words in prayer; many words and long discourses being often the occasions of wandering: hold yourself in prayer before GOD, like a dumb or paralytic beggar at a rich man's gate: let it be your business to keep your mind in the presence of the LORD. If it sometimes wander, and withdraw itself from Him, do not much disquiet yourself for that; trouble and disquiet serve rather to distract the mind, than to re-collect it; the will must bring it back in tranquillity; if you persevere in this manner, GOD will have pity on you.

One way to re-collect the mind easily in the time of prayer, and preserve it more in tranquillity, is not to let it wander too far at other times: you should keep it strictly in the presence of GOD; and being accustomed to think of Him often, you will find it easy to keep your mind calm in the time of prayer, or at least to recall it from its wanderings.

I have told you already at large, in my former letters, of the advantages we may draw from this practice of the presence of GOD: let us set about it seriously and pray for one another.

Ninth Letter

Enclosing a letter to a corresponding sister,
whom he regards with respect tinged with fear.
** His old theme concisely put.*

The enclosed is an answer to that which I received from – ; pray deliver it to her. She seems to me full of good will, but she would go faster than grace. One does not become holy all at once. I recommend her to you: we ought to help one another by our advice, and yet more by our good examples. You will oblige me to let me hear of her from time to time, and whether she be very fervent and very obedient.

Let us thus think often that our only business in this life is to please GOD, that perhaps all besides is but folly and vanity. You and I have lived above forty years in religion [i.e., a monastic life]. Have we employed them in loving and serving GOD, who by His mercy has called us to this state and for that very end? I am filled with shame and confusion, when I reflect on the one hand upon the great favours which GOD has done, and incessantly continues to do, me; and on the other, upon the ill use I have made of them, and my small advancement in the way of perfection.

Since by His mercy He gives us still a little time, let us begin in earnest, let us repair the lost time, let us return with a full assurance to that FATHER of mercies, who is always ready to receive us affectionately. Let us renounce, let us generously renounce, for the love of Him, all that is not Himself; He deserves infinitely more. Let us think of Him perpetually. Let us put all our trust in Him: I doubt not but we shall soon find the effects of it, in receiving the abundance of His grace, with which we can do all things, and without which we can do nothing but sin.

We cannot escape the dangers which abound in life, without the actual and continual help of GOD; let us then pray to Him for it continually. How can we pray to Him without being with Him? How can we be with Him but in thinking of Him often? And how can we often think of Him, but by a holy habit which we should form of it? You will tell me that I am always saying the same thing: it is true, for this is the best and easiest method I know; and as I use no other, I advise all the world to it. We must know before we can love. In order to know GOD, we must often think of Him; and when we come to love Him, we shall then also think of Him often, for our heart will be with our treasure. This is an argument which well deserves your consideration.

Tenth Letter

*Has difficulty, but sacrifices his will, to write as requested. * The loss of a friend may lead to acquaintance with the Friend.*

I have had a good deal of difficulty to bring myself to write to M. – , and I do it now purely because you and Madam desire me. Pray write the directions and send it to him. I am very well pleased with the trust which you have in GOD: I wish that He may increase it in you more and more: we cannot have too much in so good and faithful a Friend, who will never fail us in this world nor in the next.

If M. – makes his advantage of the loss he has had, and puts all his confidence in GOD, He will soon give him another friend, more powerful and more inclined to serve him.

He disposes of hearts as He pleases. Perhaps M. – was too much attached to him he has lost. We ought to love our friends, but without encroaching upon the love of GOD, which must be the principal.

Pray remember what I have recommended to you, which is, to think often on GOD, by day, by night, in your business, and even in your diversions. He is always near you and with you; leave Him not alone. You would think it rude to leave a friend alone, who came to visit you: why then must GOD be neglected? Do not then forget Him, but think on Him often, adore Him continually, live and die with Him; this is the glorious employment of a Christian; in a word, this is our profession, if we do not know it we must learn it. I will endeavour to help you with my prayers, and am yours in our LORD.

Eleventh Letter

*To one who is in great pain. God is the Physician of body and of soul. * Feels that he would gladly suffer at His wish.*

I do not pray that you may be delivered from your pains; but I pray GOD earnestly that He would give you strength and patience to bear them as long as He pleases. Comfort yourself with Him who holds you fastened to the cross: He will loose you when He thinks fit. Happy those who suffer with Him: accustom yourself to suffer in that manner, and seek from Him the strength to endure as much, and as long, as He shall judge to be necessary for you. The men of the world do not comprehend these truths, nor is it to be wondered at, since they suffer like what they are, and not like Christians: they consider sickness as a pain to nature, and not as a favour from GOD; and seeing it only in that light, they find nothing in it but grief and distress. But those who consider sickness as coming from the hand of GOD, as the effects of His mercy, and the means which He employs for their salvation, commonly find in it great sweetness and sensible consolation.

I wish you could convince yourself that GOD is often (in some sense) nearer to us and more effectually present with us, in sickness than in health. Rely upon no other Physician, for, according to my apprehension, He reserves your cure to Himself. Put then all your trust in Him, and you will soon find the effects of it in your recovery, which we often retard, by putting greater confidence in physic than in GOD.

Whatever remedies you make use of, they will succeed only so far as He permits. When pains come from GOD, He only can cure them. He often sends diseases of the body, to cure those of the soul. Comfort yourself with the sovereign Physician both of soul and body.

I foresee that you will tell me that I am very much at my ease, that I eat and drink at the table of the LORD. YOU have reason: but think you that it would be a small pain to the greatest criminal in the world, to eat at the king's table, and be served by him, and notwithstanding such favours to be without assurance of pardon? I believe he would feel exceeding great uneasiness, and such as nothing could moderate, but only his trust in the goodness of his sovereign. So I assure you, that whatever pleasures I taste at the table of my King, yet my sins, ever present before my eyes, as well as the uncertainty of my pardon, torment me, though in truth that torment itself is pleasing.

Be satisfied with the condition in which GOD places you: however happy you may think me, I envy you. Pains and suffering would be a paradise to me, while I should suffer with my GOD; and the greatest pleasure would be hell to me, if I could relish them without Him; all my consolation would be to suffer something for His sake.

I must, in a little time, go to GOD. What comforts me in this life is, that I now see Him by faith; and I see Him in such a manner as might make me say sometimes, I believe no more, but I see. I feel what faith teaches us, and, in that assurance and that practice of faith, I will live and die with Him.

Continue then always with GOD: 'tis the only support and comfort for your affliction. I shall beseech Him to be with you. I present my service.

Twelfth Letter

To the same correspondent probably, and expresses his own abiding comfort through faith.

If we were well accustomed to the exercise of the presence of GOD, all bodily diseases would be much alleviated thereby. GOD often permits that we should suffer a little, to purify our souls, and oblige us to continue with Him.

Take courage, offer Him your pains incessantly, pray to Him for strength to endure them. Above all, get a habit of entertaining yourself often with GOD, and forget Him the least you can. Adore Him in your infirmities, offer yourself to Him from time to time; and, in the height of your sufferings, beseech Him humbly and affectionately (as a child his father) to make you conformable to His holy will. I shall endeavour to assist you with my poor prayers.

GOD has many ways of drawing us to Himself. He sometimes hides Himself from us: but faith alone, which will not fail us in time of need, ought to be our support, and the foundation of our confidence, which must be all in GOD.

I know not how GOD will dispose of me: I am always happy: all the world suffer; and I, who deserve the severest discipline, feel joys so continual, and so great, that I can scarce contain them.

I would willingly ask of GOD a part of your sufferings, but that I know my weakness, which is so great, that if He left me one moment to myself, I should be the most wretched man alive. And yet I know not how He can leave me alone, because faith gives me as strong a conviction as sense can do, that He never forsakes us, till we have first forsaken Him. Let us fear to leave Him. Let us be always with Him. Let us live and die in His presence. Do you pray for me, as I for you.

Thirteenth Letter

To the same he exhorts for fuller and entire confidence in God, for body and soul.

I am in pain to see you suffer so long; what gives me some ease, and sweetens the feeling I have of your grief's, is that they are proofs of GOD's love towards you: see them in that view, and you will bear them more easily. As your case is, 'tis my opinion that you should leave off human remedies, and resign yourself entirely to the providence of GOD; perhaps He stays only for that resignation and a perfect trust in Him to cure you. Since notwithstanding all your cares, physic has hitherto proved unsuccessful, and your malady still increases, it will not be tempting GOD to abandon yourself in His hands, and expect all from Him.

I told you, in my last, that He sometimes permits bodily diseases to cure the distempers of the soul. Have courage then: make a virtue of necessity: ask of GOD, not deliverance from your pains, but strength to bear resolutely, for the love of Him, all that He should please, and as long as He shall please.

Such prayers, indeed, are a little hard to nature, but most acceptable to GOD, and sweet to those that love Him. Love sweetens pains; and when one loves GOD, one suffers for His sake with joy and courage. Do you so, I beseech you; comfort yourself with Him, who is the only Physician of all our maladies. He is the FATHER of the afflicted, always ready to help us. He loves us infinitely more than we imagine: love Him then, and seek not consolation elsewhere: I hope you will soon receive it. Adieu. I will help you with my prayers, poor as they are, and shall be, always, yours in our LORD.

Fourteenth Letter

Gratitude, for mercies to his correspondent, and measure of relief while he has himself been near death, but with consolation in his suffering.

I Render thanks to our LORD, for having relieved you a little, according to your desire. I have been often near expiring, though I was never so much satisfied as then. Accordingly I did not pray for any relief, but I prayed for strength to suffer with courage, humility, and love. Ah, how sweet is it to suffer with GOD! however great the sufferings may be, receive them with love. 'Tis paradise to suffer and be with Him; so that if in this life we would enjoy the peace of paradise, we must accustom ourselves to a familiar, humble, affectionate conversation with Him: we must hinder our spirits wandering from

Him upon any occasion: we must make our heart a spiritual temple, wherein to adore Him incessantly: we must watch continually over ourselves, that we may not do, nor say, nor think anything that may displease Him. When our minds are thus employed about GOD, suffering will become full of unction and consolation.

I know that to arrive at this state, the beginning is very difficult; for we must act purely in faith. But though it is difficult, we know also that we can do all things with the grace of GOD, which He never refuses to them who ask it earnestly. Knock, persevere in knocking, and I answer for it that He will open to you in His due time, and grant you all at once what He has deferred during many years. Adieu. Pray to Him for me, as I pray to Him for you. I hope to see Him quickly.

Fifteenth Letter

*From his death-bed. * Repeats the same exhortation to knowledge, that we may love.*

God knoweth best what is needful for us, and all that He does is for our good. If we knew how much He loves us, we should be always ready to receive equally and with indifference from His hand the sweet and the bitter; all would please that came from Him. The sorest afflictions never appear intolerable, but when we see them in the wrong light. When we see them in the hand of GOD, who dispenses them: when we know that it is our loving FATHER, who abases and distresses us: our sufferings will lose their bitterness, and become even matter of consolation.

Let all our employment be to know GOD: the more one knows Him, the more one desires to know Him. And as knowledge is commonly the measure of love, the deeper and more extensive our knowledge shall be, the greater will be our love: and if our love of GOD were great we should love Him equally in pains and pleasures.

Let us not amuse ourselves to seek or to love GOD for any sensible favours (how elevated soever) which He has or may do us. Such favours, though never so great, cannot bring us so near to GOD as faith does in one simple act. Let us seek Him often by faith: He is within us; seek Him not elsewhere. Are we not rude and deserve blame, if we leave Him alone, to busy ourselves about trifles, which do not please Him and perhaps offend Him? 'Tis to be feared these trifles will one day cost us dear.

Let us begin to be devoted to Him in good earnest. Let us cast everything besides out of our hearts; He would possess them alone. Beg this favour of Him. If we do what we can on our parts, we shall soon see that change wrought in us which we aspire after. I cannot thank Him sufficiently for the relaxation He has vouchsafed you. I hope from His mercy the favour to see Him within a few days. Let us pray for one another.

[He took to his bed two days after and died within the week.]

INTERNATIONAL BESTSELLER

The Knowledge of the Holy

by A.W. Tozer

Pages	:	136
Size	:	8x5.25 inches
Binding	:	Paperback
Language	:	English
Subject	:	Mind, Body & Spirit
ISBN	:	9789389157130

'The Knowledge of the Holy' by A.W. Tozer illuminates God's attributes—from wisdom, to grace, to merchant in doing so, attempts to restore the majesty and wonder of God in the hearts and minds of all Christians. It teaches us how we can rejuvenate our prayer life, meditate more Reverently, understand God more deeply and experience God's presence in our daily lives.

OTHER BOOKS YOU MAY LIKE

- 1984 by George Orwell, ISBN: 9789380914947
- 12 Years a Slave by Solomon Northup, ISBN: 9789390492374
- A Passage to India by E.M. Forster, ISBN: 9789354990205
- A Room of One's Own by Virginia Woolf, ISBN: 9789354990281
- A Streetcar Named Desire by Tennessee Williams, ISBN: 9788194748601
- A Wrinkle in Time by Madeleine L'Engle, ISBN: 9789354991066
- Abraham Lincoln by Lord Charnwood, ISBN: 9789380914251
- Animal Farm by George Orwell, ISBN: 9789380914701
- Annihilation of Caste by Dr B.R. Ambedkar, ISBN: 9789390492732
- Anthem by Ayn Rand, ISBN: 9789389157079
- As a Man Thinketh by James Allen, ISBN: 9788180320262
- As I Lay Dying by William Faulkner, ISBN: 9789390492381
- Believe in Yourself by Joseph Murphy, ISBN: 9789388118385
- Chanakya Neeti by Chanakya, ISBN: 9789389716276
- Civilization and Its Discontents by Sigmund Freud, ISBN: 9789387669499
- Demian by Hermann Hesse, ISBN: 9789387669567
- George Orwell Combo : Animal Farm & 1984, ISBN: 9789390492459
- Gravity by George Gamow, ISBN: 9789388118484
- Guerrilla Warfare by Ernesto Che Guevara, ISBN: 9789354990366
- How I Made $2,000,000 in the Stock Market by N. Darvas, ISBN: 9789389716283
- How to Attract Money by Joseph Murphy, ISBN: 9789388118408
- How to Develop Self Confidence by Dale Carnegie, ISBN: 9789387669000
- How to Enjoy Your Life and Your Job by Dale Carnegie, ISBN: 9789387669017
- How to Stop Worrying and Start Living by Dale Carnegie, ISBN: 9789380914817
- How to Win Friends and Influence People by D. Carnegie, ISBN: 9788180320217
- Jail Diary and Other Writings by Bhagat Singh, ISBN: 9789390492398

OTHER BOOKS YOU MAY LIKE

- Know Your Worth by NK Sondhi & Vibha Malhotra, ISBN: 9788180320231
- Lost Horizon by James Hilton, ISBN: 9789389716313
- Maneaters of Kumaon by Jim Corbett, ISBN: 9789354990731
- Mansarover 1 (Hindi) by Premchand, ISBN: 9789380914978
- Mansarover 2 (Hindi) by Premchand, ISBN: 9789380914985
- Meditation and Its Methods by Swami Vivekananda, ISBN: 9789389716320
- Meditations by Marcus Aurelius, ISBN: 9789388118736
- My Experiments with Truth by Mahatma Gandhi, ISBN: 9789387669291
- My Inventions: The Autobiography of Nikola Tesla, ISBN: 9789388118132
- One, None and a Hundred Thousand by Luigi Pirandello, ISBN: 9789389716337
- Relativity by Albert Einstein, ISBN: 9789380914220
- Reminiscences of a Stock Operator by Edwin Lefevre, ISBN: 9788194764816
- Scientific Healing Affirmations by P. Yogananda, ISBN: 9789389716344
- Selected Stories of Rabindranath Tagore by Tagore, ISBN: 9789380914770
- Siddhartha by Hermann Hesse, ISBN: 9789380914145
- Student's Encyclopedia of G.K. by GP Editors, ISBN: 9789380914190
- Success Through a Positive Mental Attitude by N. Hill, ISBN: 9789390492435
- Tales from Shakespeare by Charles Lamb & Mary Lamb, ISBN: 9789380914367
- The Art of War by Sun Tzu, ISBN: 9789380914893
- The Autobiography of a Yogi by Paramahansa Yogananda, ISBN: 9789380914602
- The Book of Enoch by Enoch, ISBN: 9789390492480
- The Diary of a Young Girl by Anne Frank, ISBN: 9789380914312
- The Dynamic Laws of Prosperity by Catherine Ponder, ISBN: 9789388118156
- The Elements of Style by William Strunk, ISBN: 9789389157123
- The Game of Life and How to Play It by Florence Shinn, ISBN: 9789387669390
- The Law of Success by Napoleon Hill, ISBN: 9788180320927

Develop your reading habit | **Gift books to your friends**

OTHER BOOKS YOU MAY LIKE

- The Light of Asia by Sir Edwin Arnold, ISBN: 9789380914923
- The Mysterious Affair at Styles by Agatha Christie, ISBN: 9789390492510
- The Origin of Species by Charles Darwin, ISBN: 9788180320453
- The Plague by Albert Camus, ISBN: 9788194764892
- The Power of Positive Thinking by Norman Vincent Peale, ISBN: 9789388118569
- The Power of Your Subconscious Mind by Joseph Murphy, ISBN: 9788180320958
- The Problem of Increasing Human Energy by Nikola Tesla, ISBN: 9789354990953
- The Prophet by Kahlil Gibran, ISBN: 9789380914022
- The Psychopathology of Everyday Life by Sigmund Freud, ISBN: 9789388118071
- The Railway Children by E Nesbit, ISBN: 9789354990960
- The Red Badge of Courage by Stephen Crane, ISBN: 9789354990977
- The Richest Man in Babylon by George S. Clason, ISBN: 9789387669369
- The Science of Getting Rich by Wallace D. Wattles, ISBN: 9788180320972
- The Sound and the Fury by William Faulkner, ISBN: 9789390492572
- The Stranger by Albert Camus, ISBN: 9789390492589
- The Sun Also Rises by Ernest Hemingway, ISBN: 9789354990984
- The World as I See It by Albert Einstein, ISBN: 9789388118125
- The Yoga Sutras of Patanjali by Patanjali, ISBN: 9789389716351
- Their Eyes Were Watching God by Zora Neale Hurston, ISBN: 9788194764885
- Think and Grow Rich by Napoleon Hill, ISBN: 9788180320255
- Thought Vibration by William Walker Atkinson, ISBN: 9789389157154
- To the Lighthouse by Virginia Woolf, ISBN: 9789390492190
- Who were the Shudras by Dr B.R. Ambedkar, ISBN: 9789354991028
- World's Best Short Stories: Volume 1 by Various Authors, ISBN: 9789390492275
- Wuthering Heights by Emily Brontë, ISBN: 9788193545898
- Zen in the Art of Archery by Eugen Herrigel, ISBN: 9789354991059

Develop your reading habit | **Gift books to your friends**

www.ingramcontent.com/pod-product-compliance
Ingram Content Group UK Ltd.
Pitfield, Milton Keynes, MK11 3LW, UK
UKHW032043260826
14628UKWH00008B/3134